Urban Cycles

A play

Michael Snelgrove

Samuel French – London
New York – Sydney – Toronto – Hollywood

CHARACTERS

Robin
Buzz
Henry
Lavinia
Fran
Wolf
Derek
Gerard
Marguerite
Clooney
Krystel

The action of the play is set in a shopping piazza

Time—the present

Description of characters

Robin. Thirties. Energetic and single-minded in his pursuit of personal glory by charitable means, although he seriously believes he is doing good quietly.

Buzz. His wife, slightly younger. Not highly intelligent. Her nickname is a joke, which she has never understood.

Henry. Sixties. Ex-Bomber Command. Stoical and resigned to his fate, which largely consists of:

Lavinia. A button-holing, fussy, well-meaning little woman, to avoid whose company a lot of people find a lot of urgent things to do elsewhere.

Fran. Forties. Divorced, rather uptight. A professional woman with never a hair out of place, or an unironed crease to be seen. Has her vulnerabilities, most of which Robin can find quite effortlessly.

Wolf. Middle to late forties, trying to be early sixties. A hygienic-looking grey German businessman with a great deal of *gravitas*. He speaks very good English. Nearly.

Derek. Thirties. A pilot. Doesn't know whether he's coming or going—presumably something of a handicap in his profession.

Gerard. Forties. A large, florid man in antiques. Self-indulgence oozes off him like sweat. Quite often as sweat, actually.

Marguerite. Middle to late thirties. A small, willowy woman who works too hard at a continental style and sensuality which ill fits the more respectable suburbs of West Sussex. The kind of middle-class siren whose perfume could knock out a rhino at a hundred yards.

Clooney. Twenties. A security guard. In reality, little more than a caretaker who worships the smart uniform and the authority he thinks it gives him.

Krystel. Twenties. Wolf's wife. A German ex-sexpot. Once thin, vibrant and sexy, she is now something of an eating, sleeping lump.

URBAN CYCLES

The less salubrious end of a shopping piazza. Three a.m. on a coldish summer's morning

The piazza was probably pleasant for a couple of years after its opening, but now has a neglected air about it. Litter is piled up in doorways, fast food packages are strewn about and there is graffiti on the concrete walls

All of the shop windows are shuttered, apart from the smallish display window of Bentley's department store. The window is next to the rear doors of the shop, which in the daytime gives access to the store from the multi-storey car park. The window is full of naked dummies—bits of arms and legs and torsos. In the midst of this Henry sits cycling away on an exercise-type bicycle. He is not pedalling very fast, and has a pipe in his mouth. The bicycle has a fixed back wheel which is attached to some sort of large mileometer display, designed for public consumption. At the moment the mileage reads "ninety-two"

A few figures in sleeping bags sit or lie around the poorly lit piazza. Krystel, a large lady, is particularly prominent, but she hardly moves throughout the play, except to roll over contentedly now and then. Buzz is also asleep in a bag, as is Wolf, whilst Lavinia sleeps upright on a bench covered by a blanket

A police siren whoops past very noisily. There is the sound of distant shouting. All the offstage noises are made slightly unreal by the hour of the day. A large dog barks considerably closer to hand. Henry cycles away, oblivious

Robin enters from the main piazza direction carrying papers, including a scrapbook. He surveys the scene, not all that happily. He looks at the recorded mileage, looks at his watch, then tries to attract Henry's attention

Robin Henry! Henry! Henry! (*He waves his arms, all to no avail*) Henry, pay attention! Look up, Henry! Henry!

We switch to Henry. The convention is that when we can hear what is being said out in the piazza we cannot hear what is being said in the window, and vice-versa. Those who cannot be heard carry on quite normally, miming when communicating. Henry has noticed Robin. He waves happily and mimes exhaustion

Henry My word, this is thirsty work, Robin!

Robin mimes incomprehension

    I could murder a pint!

Robin You must go faster, Henry!

Henry No, not long to go now!

Robin Faster! You've only got five minutes to go and you're three miles below your target sponsored mileage! Faster! (*He mimes furious cycling*)

Henry Very tough on the old B.U.M., this. Tell Lavinia to break open a lager, would you?

Robin Faster! Cycle faster!

Henry Lager. Yes. A lager! (*He smacks his lips and does a thumbs up*)

Robin If you don't hurry up we're not going to ... oh, for God's sake! (*He goes through the double doors and enters the window*)

    Fran enters, carrying a bag, which she puts down

More police sirens and flashing blue lights. More large dogs barking. The action is still in the piazza. From Henry's gestures and expressions we can tell that he doesn't like what he is hearing from Robin. Henry points at his backside. Then, shrugging, he stops cycling, takes his pipe out of his mouth, puts it away, bends over the handlebars, screws his eyes up and begins to pedal with increased energy. The increase in speed is not all that noticeable

The sleepers sleep on, stirring slightly. Krystel moans, obviously experiencing an erotic Teutonic dream

Fran looks at the window, but when she sees Robin looking at her she quickly looks away

Robin Ah. There's Fran. I think I'd better just have a word ...

Henry Is this fast enough for you?

Robin No.

Henry Tough tittie.

Robin disappears from the window. Fran is sorting stuff out of her bag. Robin appears at the doors

Robin Fran.

Fran does not look up

Fran Robin.

Robin Could I have a word?

Fran It seems to me you've had enough of those already. Most of them extremely hurtful.

Robin Yes, it's about that I wanted to . . . our earlier . . . disagreement.

Fran That wasn't a disagreement, Robin. For a disagreement to occur two points of view need to be expressed. What actually happened was that you harangued me. In point of fact.

Robin I wouldn't say harangued . . .

Fran No, I don't suppose you would.

Robin I was upset. Can't you understand that? Upset and disappointed. Bitterly disappointed.

Fran Oh, dear.

Robin Will you listen to what I'm saying to you, Fran?

Fran Certainly, Robin. As long as you don't harangue me. Because I'm not prepared to put up with that in my spare time. I get enough of it in there, at work. I often think my title—assistant manager—is, in fact, a misnomer. What I am, actually, is a walking target for constant abuse. I get taunted by the junior staff, abused by the senior management, bombarded by peremptory memos from Cheshunt, and as for the customers, I suffer language from them you wouldn't credit from people with American Express cards—so I'm not going to put up with it from you. Especially not at three o'clock on a cold Saturday morning.

Robin But surely you can understand how I felt? I mean, the mix-up over the window, Derek's non-arrival from Gatwick, Gerard and Marguerite telling me they'd be late because of the opera . . .

Fran I understand disappointment, Robin. Nobody understands it better.

Robin I wasn't getting angry for myself. I was getting angry on behalf of the group.

Fran So it was on behalf of the group that you called me an inefficient menopausal neurotic? A slacker? A waste of space? A bureaucratic catastrophe looking for somewhere to happen? Did the rest of the group vote democratically on these descriptions?

Robin Of course not. It was just a spur of the moment assessment.

Fran I see. Fine. Then we both know where we stand, don't we?

Robin I mean I was just trying to express the disappointment ... the frustration ... that everybody in the group felt because you ... we didn't get the front window.

Fran I didn't notice anybody else shouting and screaming and waving their arms at me.

Robin I'm a man of violent passions, Fran. You know that. I care deeply about this charity work, so possibly, yes, I over-react now and then. I just want things to be right. Do you understand that? Call me a perfectionist, if you like ...

Fran I've got a much better word than that.

Robin Look, can't we just forget the whole thing?

Fran I have, Robin. I've forgotten all about it. I've been home and had a good cry and a bath. I've listened to a Richard Clayderman LP and I've somehow managed to compose myself. Though how long it's going to take me to regain my self-esteem ... But I warn you, Robin Kibble: don't ever talk to me like that again, not if you and Buzz want to enjoy a normal married life in the years to come. Clear?

Robin Clear.

Fran Good.

Buzz stirs and wakes up

Buzz Hello, Fran. You're back.

Fran Full marks, Buzz.

Buzz We're all having a little sleep.

Fran So you are.

And so saying, Buzz returns to that enviable state. There is a sudden beeping noise. Wolf sits bolt upright. He turns off the alarm on his watch and struggles out of his sleeping bag. He greets Robin and Fran and starts to talk earnestly to Robin. But we go to Henry behind the window

Henry You're up, are you, Wolf? Right on the dot, naturally. How typically Teutonic. (*Pause*) Come on sausage head, get your skates on. Don't stand there gassing. My B.U.M. is completely N.U.M. (*pause*) B.

Back to the piazza

Wolf ... all I am saying, Robin, is that I ... we ... the company ... have to do some serious re-thinking about our sponsorship commitment.

Robin You don't think it's a bit late in the day to tell me this, Wolf?

Wolf On the contrary, my dear fellow, it's very early in the morning! Joke, Robin. Whatever happened to that famous British sense of humour? But back to business. Circumstances have changed. When I originally got the go-ahead from Dusseldorf we thought we should be in the front display window overlooking the central shopping piazza.

Robin I know all this, Wolf.

Wolf Please, Robin. Have the decency to allow me to finish. Where was I? (*He mutters to himself*) Serious sponsorship commit ... Dusseldorf ... Ah yes. But what is the reality we now find ourselves in, however? (*He thinks*) However, what is the reality in which we now find ourselves? Hmm. A back window, facing the multi-storey car park. Hardly propitious, Robin. Hardly propitious.

Robin The thing is, that Fran ...

Fran Don't you start on me again. I told you. The decision wasn't mine. It was taken at Area Manager's level at Up ...

Robin Yes, yes.

Fran Please don't harry me, Robin.

Robin Sorry.

Fran Right out of the blue we got a green memo from Upminster, telling us that the front window had to be given priority for a display of Swedish ultra-violet sun beds.

Robin Surely it could have waited until Monday?

Fran You don't ignore a green memo from Upminster, Robin, not even for a weekend. Careers in retailing have foundered on far less.

Robin Swedish sun beds ...

Fran What's that, Robin?

Robin Nothing, Fran. Nothing.

Fran Even if we'd sent a pink emergency requisition slip to

Advanced Forward Planning at Hemel Hempstead we couldn't have avoided putting those sun beds in the front window. No power on earth could have prevented it.

Wolf I understand all of this, Fran. But it does not change my fundamental position *vis-à-vis* our sponsorship. We manufacture and import very high quality cars here. Our image is important, especially in this town where is situated our British Headquarters. (*He thinks*) Where our British Headquarters is situated. Are. Are situated. Where our British Headquarters are situated. So we must be very careful how our name is used.

Robin It's for *charity*, for God's sake! Sorry, sorry ...

Wolf And so, because we wish to be accepted in this town, and because we are a caring, concerned company, we agree to sponsor charitable events. Your sponsored cycle ride, for example. But all may be well. Who knows? I shall have to phone my Managing Director in Dusseldorf.

Fran At this time of the morning?

Wolf Dusseldorf never sleeps, Fran. You would do well to remember that.

Fran Don't patronize me, Wolf. We're not some little banana republic.

Wolf Not yet, Fran, not yet. I shall phone from my car. Excuse me. (*He goes to his bag to look for his phone book*)

Robin Wolf's right. This window is hopeless for our purposes. Nobody comes round here except lost old age pensioners and gangs of youths waiting to mug them. And look at this window! It's full of naked women. It's embarrassing. There ought to be byelaws about it.

Fran I've apologized all I'm going to, Robin.

Robin Don't apologize to me. Apologize to all the old folk who'll die of hypothermia this winter. But then of course, flogging Swedish sun beds is much more important. I see that.

Wolf Possibly we could donate the unsold sun beds to the old folks and save ourselves all this trouble?

Robin (*laughing*) Yes, very good, Wolf. Yes ...

Wolf Actually, I was being serious. I am going to phone Dusseldorf now.

Robin And if they say no, you withdraw your sponsorship?

Wolf Dusseldorf brooks no arguments, Robin. It is the Upminster of the Federal Republic.

Robin And all the posters and display material your publicity department did for us ...

Wolf Cannot be exhibited. So it goes.

Robin (*suddenly deflating*) Wonderful.

Fran That won't do your public image much good, will it, Robin?

Robin (*sharply*) What?

Fran Nothing.

Wolf Look at our two wives here, Robin, sleeping away. Your wife, my wife, snug as two bugs in a rug, bless their little cotton sex. (*He thinks*) Socks. How little they know. (*He walks towards the window on his way to the car park*)

We switch to Henry

Henry Ah, at last. (*He sees that Wolf is walking past*) Oi! What the ...! Wolf! Wolf! You're ... Wolf!

Clooney appears from the piazza direction

The dog's barking is nearer

Clooney (*shouting*) Oi! Where do you think you're going?

Everybody except Krystel wakes up

Buzz Whaa ...?

Lavinia Oh, my goodness. ...

We go to Henry. He stops cycling and looks at the new arrival

Henry Ah! The cavalry's arrived! Put that in your meerschaum and smoke it, Fritz.

We go to the piazza

Clooney You heard me. I said where do you think you're going?

Wolf If it is any business of yours, I am going to the car park to use the phone.

Clooney There isn't a phone in the car park.

Wolf But there is in my car.

Clooney Oh. Vorsprung durch technik.

Lavinia Do you have to shout? Some of us were sleeping.

Buzz I was having a little sleep, Robin.

Clooney You're not seriously thinking of going into that car park alone, are you?

Wolf Why not?

Clooney I wouldn't, my friend. I really wouldn't. Take the word of one who knows.

Fran What are you getting at, Clooney?

Clooney Mister Clooney. That car park's a no-go area, after dark. Not even the security staff venture down there after the sun's gone down.

Buzz It sounds like that vampire film we saw, Robin.

Clooney I sometimes send Sabre down there for a sniff about and even he comes back shaking and trembling. Like dogs do when they've seen something beyond normal human parameters . . .

Buzz I had to watch it with my eyes closed, didn't I, Robin?

Clooney I wouldn't like to think what sort of nightlife gathers in that car park, lady. Nightlife did I say? Swamplife, more like. The sort that only comes out at night, to crawl around in its own slime.

Buzz I'm getting scared, Robin.

Wolf My dear man, what are you talking about?

Clooney I'm talking about the night shift, my friend. Inhabitants of the twilight zone. The plague of the zombies.

Buzz That's another film I can't watch.

Clooney We get them all down there. Dope fiends, glue sniffers, perverts. The kind of scum your sort only encounters in documentaries on Radio Four. But Sabre and me are down here on the sharp end every night. We're the ones facing up to the mess the permissive society left behind.

Fran This is West Sussex we're talking about, is it?

Lavinia Actually, Henry and I are addicts.

Clooney (*suddenly on the alert*) What?

Lavinia Radio Four addicts. And we've never come across anyone remotely like that. We've always met a very nice class of person on Radio Four.

From the car park comes the sound of skidding, as of a car chase. Bangs, crashes and shouting. The distance and the echo makes the noises seem unreal and, indeed, frightening in a vague sort of way

Robin Bloody hell.

Clooney I rest my case.

Wolf I'm sorry but I do have to phone Dusseldorf.

Clooney On your own head be it. At your own peril.

Wolf starts to go towards the car park. He turns

Wolf I don't suppose that anybody would care for a stroll to ...?

But nobody is really very keen

Clooney Sabre should be down there on patrol. He'll keep an eye out for you.

Wolf This is meant to reassure me?

Wolf goes, rather gingerly

Clooney He won't be back. Not in one piece, anyway.

Robin Don't be ridiculous. This is a civilized country.

Clooney Which newspaper have you been reading?

More noises from the car park

Kraut, is he?

Robin He's a German citizen, yes.

Clooney gives an expressive sniff. He notices something in the direction of the piazza

Clooney Look, there's my Sabre! What are you doing, boy? Ah, look, he's eating!

The dog barks and growls

Hold on, he should be down in the car park. What are you doing up here, you naughty doggy? (*Laughing*) Your mate in the car park's got no chance if Sabre's up here. What's that you're eating, Sabre? Oh no! He's at the potted plants again! Sabre, they're plastic! They're for decorative purposes only! Sabre! Now you sick that up! Do you hear me? Sick that up immediately!

Clooney moves off, concerned

Robin One man and his dog. Clooney, did you say?

Fran His friends call him Rosemary. A total idiot, but he's the only one who'll do the night shift for the money they pay.

Buzz I can see his dog, Robin. It's huge. It's like a wolf.

Fran You mean inflexible, pompous and self-opinionated?

Buzz Sssh! Krystel will hear you!

Fran She won't hear a thing. Sleeps like a log. Looks a bit like one, too, if we're being honest.

Robin Wolf told me she sleeps sixteen hours at a stretch after a really big meal.

Lavinia goes to the window to communicate with Henry

Buzz She's quite ugly for a beauty therapist, isn't she? That's what she used to be in Dusseldorf. It's funny, Wolf's much older than her, but he looks younger now she's put on all that weight. Funny, isn't it?

Robin Lavinia? Tell Henry that as soon as Wolf comes back he'll relieve him on the bike.

Henry is by now too tired to take in anything. Lavinia starts to give him Robin's message

Lavinia Robin says that Wolf will take over from you when he comes back from 'phoning Dusseldorf.

We go to Henry

Henry Where's my damned lager?

We return to Lavinia

Lavinia Robin says that ... (*She starts to mime*) Robin ... (*She jumps about, flapping her arms*)

Henry What are you doing, woman?

Lavinia Robin ... (*She repeats her display*)

Henry Do I need a pee? Yes! I'm bursting! Bursting! (*He nods*)

Lavinia takes this as a sign of comprehension

Lavinia Robin says ...

Lavinia mimes "says". Henry just stares in blank incomprehension

Wolf ... (*She mimes this. Carry on until the end of the message*)

A huge skid and a crash from the car park

Robin I wonder where that reporter and TV crew got to? I told everybody that I'd be on the box.

Buzz Perhaps they'll come tomorrow.

Robin It is tomorrow. I think I'll give them a ring first thing. Just to remind them. Publicity is our life blood.

Buzz Eight times, Lavinia.

Lavinia Eight times! Was it? Golly, I don't know where you young people get the energy. (*She thinks*) Eight times what, exactly?

Buzz Robin was on local television eight times last year.

Robin Nine, actually, Buzz.

Lavinia Eight times?

Robin Nine.

Lavinia How lovely! What a shame we haven't got one. Henry won't have it in the house. (*She carries on miming*)

Derek enters. He looks dazed

Buzz It was eight, Robin.

Robin It was nine! I watched the videos yesterday. Derek!

Derek Labyrinth. That car park's a labyrinth.

Fran Are you all right, Derek?

Derek I'm fine. I couldn't find my way around the car park. I've been driving for hours. Up the ramps. Down the ramps. Out to the exit. Back again. There's no lights on out there, you know. I'm fine. A bit tired, that's all. Only got into Gatwick half an hour ago. I'm fine. I'll be all right. Tired, you see. Flew in from Majorca. Only just got in. Gatwick, half an hour ago. I've been to Palma and back three times today, so I'm a bit ... it's the package holidays, you see? Peak season. The Kiss Me Quick and Viva Espãna brigade. They sang the birdy song all the way back. Do you know the birdy song? I do. It's driving me mad. Been to the Costa Brava and back sixteen times this week. Every flight, they sing it. (*He whistles a bit of the birdy song*) No, I'm a bit tired, that's all.

Lavinia has by now understood Henry

Lavinia Henry says that he wants relieving, Robin. He says that he's done more than his fair stint.

Robin He's still two miles short of his sponsorship target.

Lavinia He says if he's not relieved soon his B.U.M. will drop off altogether.

Fran That must have been an interesting mime.

Lavinia He's also started talking to the naked women, and that'll do his blood pressure no good at all.

Robin Derek. Derek?

Derek Yes, sorry, Robin? Dozing off.

Robin Feeling okay?

Derek Fine, Robin. Just a bit tired that's all. I've been to Palma and back three times ...

Robin Yes, yes. Feel like taking a turn?

Derek Just have a bit of a rest and I'll be all right.

Robin A turn on the bike?

Derek Turn on the bike? Fine. No problem. Yes. Probably wake me up. Be as good as a rest. (*He walks in the wrong direction*)

Robin Wrong way, Derek.

Derek Wrong way. Right.

Derek automatically turns round and walks to the doors with Robin

Robin The thing is, Henry's fallen behind on the overall sponsorship target so try to make up as much as you can, all right?

Derek Much as I can. Right.

Robin Good lad.

Derek enters the store and goes into window

Robin I don't know what I'd do without Derek. A heart of gold.

Fran And porridge for brains. Didn't you see what a state he was in?

Robin He'll be fine.

Buzz Funny to think of Derek being an airline pilot. His legs don't look long enough.

Robin That's a point. Lower the saddle, Derek. Lower the : ...

Derek has taken over from Henry. For a few moments he has been sitting on the bike pedalling, failing to notice that his feet are several inches off the pedals

Fran Is he all right, do you think?

Buzz He looked a bit dazed to me, Robin.

Robin Derek? No. He always looks like that. Dozy Derek, they used to call him at school. He'll be fine.

Henry hurries out of the door and straight past them to the piazza

Henry Nature calls ...

Henry exits, rapidly

Wolf comes on. He is not amused

Wolf This country of yours! I ask you—what kind of country is this?

Lavinia It's a Parliamentary democracy, isn't it?

Wolf That guard fellow was right.

Buzz What's the matter, Wolf?

Wolf In what other country would you be sitting in your car making a phone call—a completely empty car park, no other car in sight—when suddenly a maniac screams in, smashes into one's car, pulls forward, reverses into one's car again and drives off? Anywhere else in the world they would have stopped. But not here. Not in this dishonest apology for a country.

Buzz That's awful.

Fran Did you get a look at them?

Wolf It was very dark, but I think it was only one man. Obviously a lunatic. I had an impression of staring eyes and a fixed grin. Drunk or drug-crazed. He was a . . . what do you call them? A pleasure driver.

Fran Joyrider.

Wolf Yes.

Robin What kind of car?

Wolf What kind of . . .? It was over in a few moments, you know, Robin—and there were no lights on, of course, just as one would expect in this country.

Robin So you didn't see much?

Wolf All I can tell you is that it was a maroon Volvo 740 Super version, wheel trims, sunroof, AA badge on the front grille and a towbar on the back. Apart from this I can tell you nothing.

Robin Number?

Wolf What do you think I am, Robin? Wonderperson?

Lavinia Superman.

A dog barks loudly

Henry returns hastily

Henry Damned great dog waiting for me outside the bog. Very funny look in its eyes. I think it was on heat. Rather worrying.

Wolf And another thing—the car park is flooded! Yes! The whole second floor is flooded!

Henry What are you looking at me for?

Wolf How does one contrive to flood the second floor only of a car park?

Henry It's called British inventive genius.

Wolf The whole floor is ankle deep in water and nobody is doing a damned thing about it! What a country! How do you stand it? Abandoned shopping trolleys everywhere, the smell of I shudder to think what on the stairs and graffiti so obscene that even Krystel has to avert her eyes—and she is very broad minded. Very. Often I say to her "Welcome to Britain in the late twentieth century". And she says: "Wolf, you *are* welcome to it!" In German, of course.

Henry Nobody asked you to come over here flogging your overpriced kraut motors.

Robin Henry . . .

Wolf I must say, the British seem keen enough to buy them, Henry. Possibly because your own cars fall apart so quickly. At least in Germany we build things to last.

Henry For a thousand years?

Lavinia Henry!

Henry Well . . .

Lavinia I don't know what's got into you.

Henry And I don't know why we fought a bloody war.

Robin What did Dusseldorf say?

Wolf They were not happy when I explained to them what had happened. Not happy at all. But I talked them round.

Robin Well done, Wolf, well done!

Henry *Deutschland uber alles.*

Robin You start setting up the display now, all right?

They do so. Robin heads towards the window

Buzz We were saying that Krystel's put on a little bit of weight, Wolf.

Wolf Yes. A little. Thirteen and a half kilos to be exact. She hates this country, so she eats. It is so sad. Her body used to be . . . oh well. And she sleeps, of course. Nearly all the time. In Dusseldorf she used to wear me out, sexwise, but now . . . I tell her it is not right. It is not why I married her, so she should sleep. She is young. She should make me very happy in the bedroom. But she sleeps. And sleeps and sleeps . . . Ah! There is Derek at last! My word, he looks a little . . . what is the word you use?

Buzz Tired?

Wolf No . . .

Fran Exhausted?

Wolf Knackered. That is the word.

Henry *Knackwurst.*
Wolf You know German, Henry?
Henry Only what I've picked up in delicatessens.

Robin goes into the window and we hear him and Derek speaking

Robin So if you could just pedal a bit faster, Derek, there's a lot of ground to catch up ...
Derek No problem, Robin, no problem. (*But he is really too tired to increase the pace*)
Robin What, er ... what sort of car you driving these days, Derek?
Derek What?
Robin What sort of car?
Derek Car? Ohh ... now ... car?
Robin You must know what sort of car you drive, Derek.
Derek A red one.
Robin Maroon?
Derek Yes.
Robin Maroon Volvo?
Derek Yes. Why?
Robin Nothing. No reason. Don't mention it to Wolf, that's all. Shtum.

We go back to the piazza

Wolf I hope Derek is up to all this punishing physical exercise. He looks terribly tired.
Fran He hardly knows where he is.
Wolf This is not good in an airline pilot.
Fran Moira told me he landed at Amsterdam the other day.
Buzz What's so wrong about that?
Fran He thought it was Gatwick. Until he realized their English was too good ...
Wolf Amsterdam. ... (*He tuts and shakes his head ruefully*)
Henry Not a mistake the *Luftwaffe* would have made?
Wolf You mean *Lufthansa*?
Henry I know what I mean.
Lavinia Yes, I was saying earlier to that dreadful man, we're really very much Radio Four people, aren't we, Henry?

Return to Derek and Robin

Robin I've bought that scrapbook you said you were interested in, Derek.

Derek Oh. Lovely.

Robin Let me ... (*He holds up the scrapbook in front of Derek's nose*) There's all the usual cuttings from the local papers—that's a particularly good photo of me and Buzz, I think ...

Derek Oh yes.

Robin But there's a couple here from the nationals; from when we were on *That's Life*—remember that?

Derek Oh yes.

Robin That's us pictured with Esther and Cyril. And there's one from *The Mail on Sunday* here somewhere. ...

Derek She's left me, Robin.

Robin What's that, Derek?

Derek Moira. She's left me.

Robin Moira?

Derek Moira. My wife.

Robin Oh, Moira.

Derek Found a note stuck on the freezer with a magnetic elephant. Left me and gone to her sister's.

Robin I wouldn't worry about a little thing like that. Fit of pique I expect. They're like that, women. They have these funny turns. Buzz usually blames it on her cycle. (*He laughs*) That's a good one. Get it? Cycle.

Derek What? Oh ... (*He laughs feebly*)

Robin No, let her have a good night's sleep at her sister's. Go home in the morning and she'll be there like she's never been away.

Derek I doubt it.

Robin Why?

Derek Her sister lives in Australia.

Robin I see. But why, Derek?

Derek She married an Australian.

Robin Why would she want to leave you? That's what I can't understand. You're the ideal couple: everybody says so. I can't for the life of me think of a single, solitary reason why she'd do this to you, Derek.

Derek Sexual frustration.

Robin Sorry?

Derek It's all in the note. The one she stuck to the freezer with a magnetic camel ...

Robin Elephant.

Derek What?

Robin You said magnetic elephant.

Derek Sorry. (*He produces a note*) "Gone to Irene's in Adelaide. Australia is a young, vibrant, wide awake country, and if the daytime soaps are to be believed, Australian men are some of the most over-sexed in the world, so I'm off to give it a go. I married you because I thought airline pilots led exciting and glamorous lives. Ironic, isn't it? I might as well have married a quantity surveyor for all the excitement I've had, and I don't just mean the sex, either. On second thoughts, perhaps I do. Nothing personal, Derek, I've just had enough. Or rather, I haven't. Dinner in oven." Signed, Moira.

Robin I see . . .

Derek I used to fall asleep a lot, you see. Because of all the flying, all the package holiday flights. I'm knackered for the whole summer. I've been to Palma three times . . .

Robin Yes, yes. I know, Derek.

Derek So when I get home I'm in no state to . . . I get home tonight, what do I find? This note, this bloody note, stuck to the freezer with a magnetic whale . . .

Robin Elephant.

Derek What?

Robin Nothing.

Derek That's what it comes down to. Twelve years of marriage . . . and this is what it's reduced to . . .

A tricky pause. Derek starts to cry. Robin shuffles in an awkward and embarrassed fashion

Go to the piazza

Lavinia Brian Redhead.

Henry John Timpson.

Lavinia Sue Macgregor and Margaret Howard.

Henry Grand girls.

Lavinia Alistair Cooke. The week's good cause, of course. We always give to that, even though money is scarcer since we retired. We find the radio such a comfort as we enter the twilight years. It's like asking a lot of very good friends into your living room. Henry won't have a television. Refuses to have one in the house.

Henry Not me. You.

Lavinia No, Henry, you're the one who's against it.

Henry I'd quite like one. Give me something to look at of an evening instead of staring at your ugly mug.

Lavinia In that case, we'll go out and get one on Monday! Why not? We may as well live a bit in our old age.

Henry I'm only sixty-six!

Lavinia Of course, what I miss are the evenings we used to spend with the boys, sitting around the wireless, all cosy and snug. But since Toby and Royston left home . . . it's not the same with just two of us, is it, Henry?

Henry Oh, I don't know.

Lavinia It's *definitely not* the same, Henry.

Henry No. It's even more boring.

By now the display boards are up

We go to Robin and Derek, who is now in quite a state but, encouraged by Robin, still pedalling

Derek Paella!

Robin Sorry, Derek?

Derek The meal she left in the oven! Paella! Rotten, stinking paella! As if I don't get enough of that sort of muck in Palma! She knows I hate it, Robin! I hate it! I hate bloody paella!

Robin Steady on, Derek, steady on!

We go to the piazza

Buzz Look at those two in there! I expect Robin's telling one of his jokes. Derek's always liked Robin's jokes. Look at him— tears streaming down his face!

We go to the window. Derek is in floods of tears. Robin really can't handle it

Robin Don't, Derek. Please . . . ummmm . . . look on the bright side.

Derek Bright side? What bright side? There is no bright side! How would you feel if Buzz suddenly left you?

Robin looks out at Buzz, who waves brightly at him. He thinks. The thought is obviously not all that unpleasant

Robin (*slightly ruefully*) Yes . . . no, what I meant was, look on the bright side—you're bang on target for your sponsorship mileage! Excuse me ...

Robin exits from the window, leaving Derek in a bit of a state. The others have just finished putting up the boards

Wolf There!

Robin Well done, Wolf!

Buzz They're lovely, aren't they, Fran? I love this sticky stuff. It feels very sensual.

Robin Good work, Wolf. (*He looks at the display*) Just one thing ...

Wolf Yes, Robin?

Robin Umm, don't know how to put this ... but the name of your firm is plastered all over it and I can't see any mention of us.

Wolf Us?

Robin The group. Us. The Muncaster Philanthropists.

Wolf Down here. See? (*He points to a tiny corner of one of the boards*)

Robin No, you don't seem to be grasping my point, Wolf. The boards are all plastered in glossy photographs of your cars and advertising stuff for your firm. ...

Wolf This is so.

Robin And we get a tiny mention down here. I thought it was the other way round. I thought ...

Wolf I think that we are not understanding each other very well here, Robin. My firm is sponsoring the cycle marathon. We have paid money to your excellent charities for this. But we must have some return, do you see? We are a commercial company. We do nothing for nothing. Does that sound correct? We naturally expect something from you. For heaven's sake, Robin, we are not a charity.

Robin But you are prepared to exploit charity for your own purposes?

Wolf Which of us is not, Robin?

Robin Me, for one.

Wolf You? What about your fanatical search for personal publicity?

Robin Now, just a minute ...

Wolf My dear Robin, you don't for a moment believe that you are not doing all this merely to boost your own massive ego? Everybody here knows this.

Pause

Robin My what?
Wolf Your rampaging egg.
Fran Ego.

Wolf is mortified at his mistake

Robin Personal pub . . . Ego? Me? (*He makes a decision*) Your turn
on the bike, I think, Wolf.

A moment between them. Wolf gives in

Wolf Certainly, Robin. Of course. My pleasure entirely. (*He
moves towards the doors*)

*As Wolf moves there is a strange unearthly noise from the car park.
They all turn to look, amazed. The noise is joined by a dog howling.
It is quite scary*

Buzz Robin. . . .

   Clooney rushes on

Clooney You've heard it, then?
Fran What is it?
Clooney I've heard every kind of noise from down that car park,
believe me, but I've never heard anything like this. Even Sabre
looks worried.
Buzz It's horrible.
Lavinia It's tortured.
Wolf It's Wagner.
Clooney Wagner?
Wolf Richard Wagner. The composer.
Clooney Oh, *Wagner!*

Wolf goes in through the doors

The sound gets closer and closer

   *Eventually Gerard and Marguerite enter. Gerard is in evening
   dress with a flowing cloak. Marguerite is in a splendid silk and
   taffeta number. They are singing a duet from some Wagner thing
   or other, which climaxes as they enter*

*Luckily we do not hear this, for as soon as they are on we go to Wolf
and Derek in the window. They are swapping over on the bike*

Wolf Gerard and Marguerite have arrived at last.
Derek Batman and Robin.
Wolf Is this the same as Wonderperson?

We go to the piazza, possibly to catch the last of the duet, which they are making a real song and dance of. Everybody is faintly embarrassed

Gerard And never let it be said that we do not know how to make an entrance.
Fran I don't think there's any danger of that.
Marguerite Are we late? Gosh, Gerard, I think we are. I think we are awfully late. Robin's going to give us a slap on the wrists, I can tell.
Gerard Robin, slap us not. Instead chastise the magnificent but prolix Herr Wagner. He would compose such very long operas.
Marguerite We've been at the Garden.
Clooney Whose garden?
Marguerite Covent Garden.
Clooney In the fruit and veg trade, are you?
Gerard (*ignoring him*) *Gotterdammerung.*
Clooney Language.
Gerard Magnificent. Quite magnificent. And so refreshing to hear it sung in the original German. None of this terrible translation nonsense. We've sung the score all the way home in the car. We must have looked extraordinary, darling, speeding down the motorway in the Merc, singing like two lovebirds ...
Marguerite We must.
Gerard Imagine us, if you will, sitting in the car, singing. *Du singst mit mir, meine liebeling?*

Together they sing the duet again. This time it is excruciatingly embarrassing

We go to Derek and Wolf. Wolf is now on the cycle

Wolf Tell me, Derek, do you think that Gerard is ... what is the word?
Derek A prat?
Wolf It is a good word.
Derek He'd win prizes.
Wolf Also I hate Wagner. So bloody German.

We go to the piazza. Gerard and Marguerite finish. There is a very embarrassed pause

Buzz I love your dress, Marguerite. Is it acrylic?

Marguerite Raw silk, Buzz darling.

Gerard We should have been earlier but there was a technical hitch, which meant that Valhalla was two hours late arriving. I don't believe any symbolism was intended.

Buzz What was it you saw?

Marguerite *The Twilight of the Gods*, sweetie. Have a look at the programme. It's all very Germanic and gloomy. One order ending to be replaced by another, that sort of thing. Part of Wagner's Ring Cycle.

Buzz Oh. (*Pause*) Who's that by, then?

Gerard Unfortunately we missed our customary champagne and smoked salmon sandwiches at the interval, and so . . . (*From the depths of his cloak he produces two bottles of champagne and a huge tub of sandwiches*) We brought them with us!

Lavinia How lovely!

Buzz Champagne! I love champagne. We never have champagne, do we, Robin?

Fran Nothing but the best, Marguerite.

Marguerite Krug. Twenty-eight pounds a bottle, but then what's mere money where pleasure's concerned?

Gerard Shall we, *ma cherie*?

Marguerite *Certainement, mon amour.*

Henry I'm fond of a drop of champagne.

Marguerite We adore it.

Henry Yes, always liked a drop of champagne.

Gerard and Marguerite set themselves up in a corner and proceed to open champagne and consume sandwiches with no thought for the others, who look on enviously

We go to the window

Derek Champagne at a quarter to four in the morning. The way some people live.

Wolf Conspicuous consumption, Derek. The curse of our age.

Derek looks at him

   Cars are different. Cars are necessities.

Derek wanders out of the window and sits in the piazza staring into space. We go to the piazza. Robin moves over to Gerard

During the following Henry wanders to the window and goes in

Robin Gerard? Could I have a word . . .?

Gerard Yes, Robin? What can I do for you?

Robin Do you think . . . I mean, would you say . . . I wonder if you think—that's you and Marguerite—I mean, you don't think I do all this just to make myself look important, do you? At all?

Marguerite In what way, sweetie?

Robin You know, getting into the papers, on television, that sort of thing.

Gerard Nothing wrong in a bit of self-publicity, old son.

Robin You do think it, then?

Gerard Let's just say that you have a certain . . . reputation in the town, Robin.

Robin What?

Gerard How did a member of the Chamber of Commerce put it to me? Ah yes. "Robin Kibble," he said, "the man who gets more public exposure than a nipple on Page Three!"

Gerard and Marguerite laugh immoderately. Robin doesn't

Robin (*fighting to control his temper and just about succeeding*) Yes. I see. If you'd like to get changed fairly soon, Gerard?

Gerard Changed, Robin? Whatever do you mean?

Robin Into something more suitable. For cycling.

Gerard Cycling? I'm really not following you here, old love. You actually expect me to cycle?

Robin Yes.

Marguerite But Robin, sweetie, Gerard is a patron of the group.

Robin I know that.

Marguerite You surely can't expect any more of the man.

Gerard As a patron, I give two hundred pounds a year, Robin. I do expect a few perks. I certainly don't expect to have to do anything.

Robin I just thought you'd want to take your turn. Do your bit.

Marguerite Do his bit? Oh Robin, lover, you do have such a lovely turn of phrase.

Gerard I'm sorry, Robin, old lad, but after four hours of Wagner, smoked salmon sandwiches and the best part of a bottle of Krug

I doubt that I could do my bit, even if I knew what it meant.

Robin Right. OK. Fine.

Marguerite (*slobbering over Gerard*) Besides, if you exhaust him now, he'll have no energy left for doing his bit later on ... (*She sticks her tongue in his ear*)

Gerard Oh, ho ho ...

Gerard and Marguerite laugh and smooch

We go to the window

Henry About what I said earlier ...

Wolf Forget it, Henry. I have.

Henry I haven't. Like to clear the air. You keep going on about Dusseldorf. You like Dusseldorf, do you?

Wolf I like it, yes. It's where I work when I am in Germany. Head Office. Factory. Very nice place.

Henry Still down by the railway marshalling yards, is it?

Wolf Why, yes. You know it?

Henry Oh yes. I know Dusseldorf very well, as a matter of fact. Flown over it many times.

Wolf How very pleasant.

Henry You think so? Actually, not so pleasant from the Bomb Aimer's seat of a Lancaster.

Wolf doesn't quite know what to say

Small world, isn't it?

We go to the piazza

Fran Why do you take it from them? I wouldn't take it from them.

Buzz Nor would I.

Robin You do take it from them. You're always going round there.

Buzz They've got lovely things in their house. I like touching lovely things. You never give me any lovely things to touch, Robin ...

Fran I'll say something if you won't.

Robin You said quite enough earlier, thank you very much.

Fran What do you mean?

Robin I haven't forgotten. My public image. I remember.

Fran What do you expect, if you can't open the local paper

without finding a pull-out supplement about you in it? I thought
that was what you wanted.

Robin People have got the wrong impression of me. I do this
because I'm a caring person. I am. Very caring. Aren't I, Buzz?
Buzz?

Buzz opens her mouth

We go to the window

Wolf I really don't understand why you do this, Henry. The
charity work, I mean, because you really are the most unchari-
table fellow I have ever met. The others I understand but you . . .
somehow you are not the type.

Henry If it's got anything to do with you, which I doubt, I'll tell
you: I'm a doer. Always have been. In my time I've played golf,
cricket, snooker, bowls, ping pong, tiddlywinks—you name it,
I've played it. I've been a morris dancer, an amateur actor, a glee
club singer. For a while I was fifth reserve for a barber's shop
quartet. I've collected stamps, dug Roman ruins, chaired poetry
circles and chucked in my two pen'north at the numismatic club.
I even went so far as to join the St. John's Ambulance on a
temporary basis. You see? I'm a doer. I have to be doing.
(*Pause*) In fact, anything to avoid those blasted evenings round
the wireless with Lavinia and our twee sons.

Wolf I thought you only had two?

Henry It was hell on earth. I'd even have joined the Masons to
escape that, except I wasn't asked. You're not a Mason, by
any chance? No? Oh, well. Hello. What's going on?

*And indeed, everybody outside seems to be staring towards the car
park in some alarm. We go to the piazza. Whatever Buzz has said to
Robin has not gone down well and he is sulking in a corner*

*There is a lot of noise coming from the car park. Shouts, manic
laughter, screams*

Clooney Oh yes. It's started. They've arrived.

Marguerite Who've arrived?

Clooney It's either the Hell's Angels or the vagrants. If it's both,
we're really in trouble.

Gerard I can hear women down there.

Marguerite Control yourself, darling . . .

Fran Girls, more like.

Clooney I shudder to think what's going on down there. Doesn't bear imagining.

Marguerite Aren't you going to do anything?

Clooney Me?

Gerard Isn't that what you're paid for?

Clooney Sabre!

Barking from offstage

Car park! Seek and destroy! Good boy!

More barking from offstage, receding into the distance. There is a red glow beginning to come from the car park

He'll sort them out. I haven't fed him for four days. The first sign of red meat and he'll go mad.

Gerard Is that fire?

Clooney Yes. They quite often light fires down in the basement. They barbeque ... things. (*Darkly*) Don't ask what ...

Fran Don't the police object?

Clooney The police? You won't catch the police going down there after dark, lady. What? Get out of their nice warm panda cars? I told you, it's an agreed no-go area down there after dark.

Fran I think somebody ought to do something about it. It's disgraceful in the middle of a town like this where everybody pays their rates.

Clooney Opening your eyes to a few realities now, are we?

Fran Oh shut up, Clooney. If you weren't in that uniform you'd be indistinguishable from them down there. Prancing about here like an anaemic Rambo ...

Clooney I'm warning you—don't mess with me, sweetheart.

Fran Oh, push off, Rosemary! (*She sits down*)

Derek is by now asleep with his eyes open. Suddenly Wolf leaps off the cycle screaming in agony, which we can't hear. He clutches his leg and writhes about on the floor. Henry looks at him

Buzz What's Wolf doing? He is funny. I thought the Germans weren't supposed to have a sense of humour but he creases me up! Robin, look at Wolf!

We go to the window

Henry Something wrong?

Wolf My hamstring! My hamstring has snapped again! GOTT IN HIMMEL!

Henry Oh, dear.

Wolf Well, fetch somebody, dumkoff! Do something!

Henry Yes.

Henry lights his pipe quite carefully and saunters out of the window

We go to the piazza

Buzz What's the matter, Robin? Don't you think Wolf's funny?

Robin My own wife ... the woman who I thought was my mainstay, my prop in times of crisis and doubt. Even you.

Buzz I don't know what I said.

Robin You know. You know ...

Buzz Oh, that. All I said was that you liked being a minor local celebrity. And you do.

Robin Can't you see any further than the end of your own nose? Don't you know me at all?

Buzz Of course I do. I think I do. As much as anyone can know anybody else.

Robin is struck by this unexpected vein of philosophy

Robin What do you mean—minor?

Lavinia I hope your pooch is up to dealing with this.

Robin Local?

Clooney He is. He is, don't you worry. Oh yes. I think he is.

Henry saunters out of the doors

Henry Our Teutonic friend appears to have met with an accident. Hamstring, he says.

Robin I've been on national television.

Henry (*with a "Colditz" accent*) Hammschstring. Wonder if you can buy it in a delicatessen?

Fran and Lavinia go inside to help. Robin goes to Derek

Robin Derek? Derek? I want to ask you a question. (*He passes his hand in front of Derek's face*)

Henry Asleep with his eyes open. Used to see a lot of it when we came back from bombing raids over the Ruhr. He's dog tired.

Barking from the car park

Down, Rover.

Robin Well, that's it. I give up. What's the point? Everything I do is obviously misunderstood. That's it! That's me done! Somebody else can take the responsibility of . . . why is there nobody on that bike? Why is the bike vacant? What's happened to Wolf? Never mind. (*He moves towards Gerard*) Gerard—get on that bike.

Gerard On yours, pal.

Robin (*whispering fiercely*) You've got ten seconds to get on that bike, Gerard, or the little matter of your Patronage donation will become public knowledge. All right, old love?

A moment of unabashed venom between them, then Gerard decides to make the best of a bad job. He stands up with a great flourish and removes his cloak

Gerard (*in a dreadful and embarrassing Noël Coward impression*) I have to go, my darling. But don't forget, I love you so terribly, terribly much.

Marguerite You will hurry back, won't you, Gobbles? I'm simply incomplete without you.

Gerard Miss me?

Marguerite Awfully.

Gerard Kiss-kiss.

They kiss horribly noisily and with a great flourish

Henry And yet they say Romance is dead.

Fran Gobbles?

Gerard strides manfully to the doors, Robin beside him, giving advice. Gerard tosses his cloak at Henry as he passes. He sweeps past the others as they bring Wolf out. He is in some pain. They lay him down on a bench

Lavinia Give me that blanket, Henry.

She means Gerard's cloak. Henry gives it to her and she covers Wolf in it

Henry Ah. The proverbial Wolf in creep's clothing.

Lavinia What?

Henry Nothing.

Clooney I hope Sabre's all right. Do you think he's all right?

Buzz Of course he is. He's got all those teeth and everything.

Clooney It's just that when he gets worked up he tends to roll over wanting his tummy tickled.

Gerard is by now ensconced on the bike in full opera gear, pedalling away. Robin is at his side giving advice

Marguerite Don't we all, darling? Oh, look at Gerard! Doesn't he look sweet!?

Fran If you like blancmange on a bike.

Marguerite Gerard! Poppet! (*She waves*) What a doll.

We go to the window

Robin Try to get into some sort of rhythm or you'll strain something like Wolf.

Gerard When I want your advice I'll ask for it, pal. (*He sings "The Ride Of The Valkyries" rhythmically and cycles in time with it*)

Robin Look, Gerard, it had to be said. The fact is that you and Marguerite haven't paid your Patrons' contributions for two years now.

Gerard I call it a bit underhand blackmailing me with it.

Robin Blackmail's a dirty word, Gerard.

Gerard So's what I think of you, old lad.

We go to the piazza. Fran, Lavinia and Henry are tending Wolf. Clooney is looking anxiously at the car park. Derek is still zonked out. Buzz and Marguerite are near the window talking

Marguerite This? You don't want to know, darling.

Buzz I do.

Marguerite Seven hundred.

Buzz You're joking!

Marguerite A present from Gerard.

Buzz Robin never buys me presents.

Marguerite Gerard said it was either this or a new Golf cabriolet this summer but I couldn't have both. I had both.

We go to the window

Gerard It's all right for you with your thriving little photocopying business, oh yes. But nobody wants antiques. Not the ones I sell anyway.

Robin Don't give me that. Those opera tickets must have cost you an arm and a leg.

Gerard No. Just the use of an American Express card which I can't afford to repay next month.

Robin You ought to learn to live within your means like the rest of us.

Gerard I can live within my means. It's my bloody wife out there who can't.

We go to the piazza

Buzz Rewards? What do you mean, exactly—rewards?

Marguerite You know—for being nice to him, doing him favours ...

Buzz You mean weeding the garden? Washing his car, that sort of thing ...?

Marguerite I mean special little favours. In bed. Out of it, too, quite often. Well, you have to get what you want, somehow. We all have our little ways. Presumably you've got yours. Somewhere. After all, how are we going to get what we want if we don't give them what they want? It's really very simple.

We go to the window

Robin You accuse me of publicity-seeking: what about the articles I've seen in the local rag where you've specifically mentioned that you're a Patron of the group? It makes you look good, doesn't it? Helps business.

Gerard And I need every penny, believe me.

Robin It's a bit hypocritical, wouldn't you say? Not paying your dues but getting all the credit?

Gerard Oh, go and take a funny run, little man.

Robin Who are you calling little?

Gerard Bloody little provincial oik.

Robin jerks Gerard off the bike. They scuffle

We go to the piazza. The barking is now frantic and is mixed with whimpers of pain. Laughter and shouts of delight

Clooney Sabre! They've got Sabre! They've got him! My God, what am I going to do?

Fran How about trying to rescue him?

Clooney I can't go in there! I'm authority. I represent everything they hate. They'd tear me apart. What are they doing to my little doggy?!

Henry I've never tasted Alsatian kebab. Bit tough, I should think.

The howls have become excruciating. Clooney is in an agony of indecision and close to tears with impotent rage

Clooney Why won't they give me a gun!? I've begged the Management to give me a shooter! If they'd give me a Magnum forty-four I could waste these scum in ... oh, Sabre ... Sabre! (*He bursts into tears*)

Derek suddenly stands up with a loud, incoherent cry

Fran Derek ...?

Derek I'll go.

Buzz You, Derek?

Derek I can't sit here and listen to an animal in pain. Anyway— what have I got to lose? Eh? What have I got to lose?

He strides off to the car park

Henry Good Lord.

Marguerite God, how bloody sexy! I feel quite turned on. Derek of all people!

Henry Fool woman.

Fran crosses to the window, goes in and separates Robin and Gerard

Lavinia (*to Clooney*) I hope you'll see this as an example, young man.

Buzz He looked a bit like a shorter Clint Eastwood when he walked off like that, didn't he? It's a shame about his legs.

We go to the window

Fran Derek's gone off to the car park to rescue Clooney's dog!

Robin Oh no ... what about the sponsorship target?

We go to the piazza

Clooney My little Sabre ...

We go back to the window

Robin We'll have to go after him. Get up, you!
Gerard Barbarian . . . the age of the barbarian is with us. . . .

But Robin has not waited. He is out on the piazza

Robin We've got to go in after Derek. He's a vital member of the team. And, what's more, it's his bike!

Fran fetches Gerard and explains it all to him

Wolf This is impossible. I am injured. I cannot move! What . . .!

For one moment in the play Henry moves swiftly across the stage, grabs Wolf, pulls him to his feet and drags him into formation

Henry Dusseldorf expects. Blood and Iron! *Storm und Drang! Wiener und schnitzel!*
Fran I'm going to phone Cheshunt. I'm not being held responsible for any damage to the store.
Robin That's the bottom line, is it, Fran? There's public spirit in action!

Quite deliberately Fran walks across to him, looks at him coolly and knees him in a delicate place

Ooof!
Fran Stick that in your scrap book, Bob Geldorf!

Fran disappears into the store

Buzz Robin!
Robin I'm all right. Gorrr. . . . I'm all right! You men—grab any weapon you can, anything to hit them with.

The men all grab various objects ranging from bits of wood to half-eaten french loaves

Clooney, you too. Clooney!
Clooney My little Sabre! I've had him since he was a puppy . . .
Henry He'll be no good to anyone. Funked it. Pansy boy, underneath it all, shouldn't be surprised. Always are, the mouthy ones.
Robin The four of us, then. Right.
Marguerite I'm awash with desire for you all. Gerard, lovie, whatever special little favour you want tonight, it's yours, no strings attached . . .
Gerard Will you shut up, woman! Look at me—I'm terrified! I am

sweating with fear and all you can think about is your insatiable bloody sexual appetite!

Marguerite Gerard . . . you spoke to me roughly!

Gerard Just for once in your life will you keep that oversized gob of yours firmly closed?

Marguerite bursts into tears and rushes off towards the front entrance

Lavinia Good luck, Henry. This takes me back to 'forty four. When your squadron used to go off on a sortie. Remember?

Henry Er . . . yes.

Lavinia And I used to stand at the end of the runway with my boobies bared so if you baled out and got taken prisoner you'd have something nice to remember me by.

Henry That's enough, dear.

Wolf Surely beats Radio Four, Henry.

Buzz What shall I do if you need hospital treatment, Robin? Do I go private or let the National Health take you?

Robin Let's go.

Robin, Wolf, Gerard and Henry march off

Clooney is still in tears, Lavinia and Buzz watch the men's progress. Suddenly there is an almighty commotion from the car park. It sounds like a pitched battle. They watch, horrified

Lavinia Oh dear!

Buzz I hope Robin's kept his BUPA contributions up.

After a few moments Henry, Robin and Gerard stagger back. They are bloodied and rather the worse for wear

Clooney I told you! I told you that scum would have you!

Henry Scum be damned! This is your blasted dog!

Clooney Sabre! Is my little Sabre all right? Did they torture him?

Robin They weren't torturing him at all, you clown! They were feeding him sausages from their barbeque. The poor bloody thing was starving. Rolling over with his damned great paws in the air . . .

Clooney Aaah!

Gerard But then Derek grabbed him and he went mad. Knocked

their barbeque into a skip of rubbish. Now the whole basement's on fire and it's spreading here.

Fran And Derek?

Henry Wandered off. Don't know where.

Clooney What about my little Sabre?

A mad barking from the main piazza

Sabre! Good boy! I'll set off the alarms. Sabre! Sabre! It's a red
alert, Sabre! Yes, it is! A red alert at last!

Clooney runs off happily

Henry I don't know about you but I'm off before that lot get
driven up here by the fire. They are not amused.

They make preparations to depart

Buzz Where's Wolf?

Henry Leg finally gave way, so he hopped it through the basement
into the street. I don't know. Makes you think, all this.

Robin What?

Henry Good works. (*He laughs gruffly*) Look at us.

*They do, for a moment, until the noise from the basement gets worse
and seems nearer*

Robin Time we were gone.

Robin and Henry wearily troop off towards the main piazza

The fire burns. There are noises from offstage

*Somehow, Derek appears in the window. He is in a very bad state,
hardly knowing what he is doing. He looks at the bike, then at the
target total. He gives a huge sigh, then mounts the bike and starts
to pedal very, very slowly*

*Ominous shadows appear from the car park and wait, apparently
watching*

One of the bundles on stage stirs. It is Krystel

*The main Lights snap off and red emergency lights come on. In the
eerie red glow Krystel's features are hardly distinguishable. She sits
up*

Krystel Wolf? Where are you, Wolf? I'm hungry, Wolf. Where is everybody being, please? What is all this wretched noise making? I wish only to sleep. To eat and sleep. Was is das? (*She has noticed Gerard's and Marguerite's programme. She picks it up and looks at the title page*) Ah! Gotterdammerung! (*With a great effort*) The ... Twilight ... of the Gods ...

But before she can complete the translation there is a sudden earsplitting alarm of sirens and bells

The shadows come nearer

Derek cycles, oblivious to all

The Lights fade to a Black-out

FURNITURE AND PROPERTY LIST

On stage: WINDOW
Exercise bicycle
Mileometer
Pieces of dummies

PIAZZA
Benches
Display boards in a pile
Carriers of food etc, including French bread
Pieces of wood
Rubbish strewn around

Off stage: Bag (**Fran**)

Personal: **Robin**: watch, papers including a scrapbook
Henry: pipe
Wolf: watch, sleeping bag
Krystel: sleeping bag
Buzz: sleeping bag
Lavinia: blanket
Derek: note
Marguerite: programme from Covent Garden
Gerard: 2 bottles of champagne, tub of sandwiches

LIGHTING PLOT

One exterior: a shopping piazza. No practical fittings required

To open:	Early morning light	
Cue 1	**As Fran enters** *Flashing blue police lights*	(Page 2)
Cue 2	**Clooney**: "Seek and destroy. Good boy." *Red glow from car park, increasing throughout play*	(Page 26)
Cue 3	**Robin** and **Henry** exit *Fire glow increases*	(Page 34)
Cue 4	**Krystel** stirs *Main lights snap off. Red emergency lights come on*	(Page 34)
Cue 5	**Derek** cycles, oblivious *Fade to Black-out*	(Page 35)

EFFECTS PLOT

MADE AND PRINTED IN GREAT BRITAIN BY
LATIMER TREND & COMPANY LTD PLYMOUTH

MADE IN ENGLAND